Table of Contents

The Little Bighorn 1

Origins of the Campaign 2

Great Sioux War 6

Sun Dance 8

Battle of the Rosebud 10

Battle of the Little Bighorn 13

Custer's Fight 23

Benteen goes to Reno 35

The Great Sioux Reservation 41

The Battlefield Today 43

Work Cited 45

The Little Bighorn

Battle of the Little Bighorn by Kurz and Allison (Library of Congress)

The year of 1876 is remembered for many reasons. Among them, Colorado became the 38th state, and Mark Twain published his book *"The Adventures of Tom Sawyer"*; however, the most prominent event that took place that year happened on the bluffs surrounding the Little Bighorn River. Lieutenant Colonel George Armstrong Custer and his 7th cavalry were massacred on the rolling hills of southeastern Montana. More than 250 U.S soldiers died. The battle of the Little Bighorn is the most recognized victory for the Plains Indians.

Origins of the Campaign

Custer's troops in the Black Hills expedition (National Archives)

In the sweaty summer of 1874, a wagon train of more than 1,000 soldiers lumbered through the heat of the Black Hills in present-day South Dakota. Leading the expedition was the famous Civil War commander Lieutenant Colonel George Armstrong Custer. Their objective was to find a location for a new fort, but they would find a lot more than that.

Custer and his men were marching straight through the Great Sioux Indian Reservation. The expedition was a violation of the Fort Laramie treaty of 1868, in which the government promised the Sioux Indians that U.S. troops would never be sent onto their reservation lands.

Custer and his bear 1874

Although Custer's expedition went through lush forest filled with fresh air and plentiful game, the most important event during the expedition was the discovery of gold in the Black Hills. Custer sent messengers to Fort Abraham Lincoln to spread the news. At the time, he did not think that he had broken treaty, nor that the discovery of gold would cost him his life.

General George Armstrong Custer by (Library of Congress)

"There is no doubt as to the existence of various metals throughout the hills. ... [And] examinations at numerous points confirm and strengthen the fact of the existence of gold in the Black Hills."   -George Armstrong Custer

The news spread like a wildfire. Back east, the word "GOLD" was printed in every newspaper. Hundreds of miners began flocking west, into the reservation lands, in violation of the 1868 treaty. The army was deployed to stop the relentless flood of prospectors. The soldiers burned wagons and escorted dozens of miners off the reservation, but they kept coming.

Portrait of Sioux Chief Sitting Bull by Catherine Weldon (Hulton Archive)

When the government offered to buy the Black Hills, the Indians refused. The Sioux Chief Crazy Horse said, "One does not sell the earth upon which the people walk." Chief Crazy Horse, the great spiritual leader Sitting Bull, and hundreds of followers left the reservation and scattered across the open plains of Wyoming and Montana to hunt buffalo. As more miners moved in, more Indians left the reservation and joined Sitting Bull.

President Ulysses S. Grant knew he had to get the Indians back on the reservation. In a meeting in the White House to solve the Indian crisis, the president decided that the army would no longer enforce treaty obligations. Any Indians who would not report to the government Indian agencies by January 31, 1876, would be deemed "hostile". The army would then be sent out to bring them back by force.

Sitting Bull and his followers spent the cold winter 1875 far from the reservation. When the deadline passed, not one Indian reported to the agencies. The United States Government declared war on Sitting Bull and his "hostile" followers. The Great Sioux War officially began.

General Sheridan's three-pronged assault plan

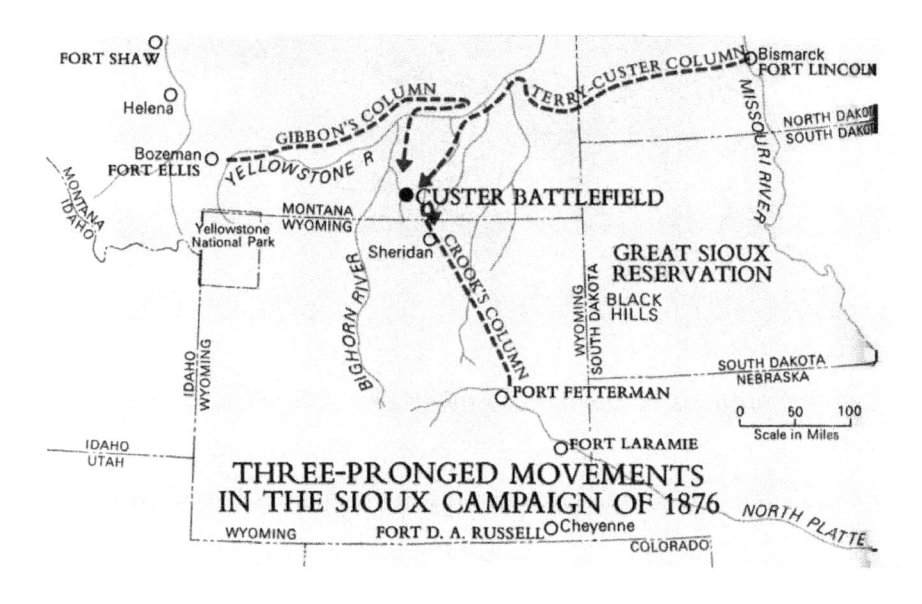

THREE-PRONGED MOVEMENTS IN THE SIOUX CAMPAIGN OF 1876

Great Sioux War

The government tasked Civil War General Philip Sheridan to plan for the coming war. He decided that a three-pronged assault would be most effective. Sheridan would split his troopers into three columns. The first column, commanded by General George Crooke, would march north from Fort Fetterman. The second column, commanded by Colonel John Gibbon, would march east from Fort Ellis; the third column, commanded by General Alfred Terry, would march west from Fort Abraham Lincoln. With Terry went 600 soldiers of the 7th cavalry commanded by Colonel George Custer.

Officers of the 7th Cavalry, many of these men would die at the Little Bighorn, Custer stands (without hat) at the bottom left (Little Bighorn National Monument) 1873

In the late spring of 1876, the three columns departed from their forts. Nobody knew exactly where the Indians were, but they were certain that one of the columns would find them.

On the frigid morning of March 17, a detachment from General Crooke's first column spotted a Cheyenne camp on the Powder River. The cavalrymen quickly made an attack. After a short but spirited fight, the camp was abandoned.

"Women screamed. Children cried for their mothers. Old people tottered and hobbled away to get out of reach of the bullets singing among the lodges. Braves seized whatever weapons they had and tried to meet the attack..." -Wooden Leg

Battle of the Little Bighorn by Elk Ebner (Little Bighorn Battlefield National Monument)

Sun Dance

Much like dozens of others, the young 18-year-old warrior, Wooden Leg, abandoned his village; now they were left with nothing. Behind them was the distant glow of burning teepees. The Cheyenne refugees made their way to Sitting Bull's camp at Rosebud Creek in Montana. The chief welcomed them with open arms.

Not long after that, Sitting Bull held a Sundance. The Sundance was the most important spiritual ceremony of the year.

In a traditional sun dance, the dancer would stick two strips of buffalo hide through his chest skin and dance around a pole, sometimes for days. Instead of this, Sitting Bull cut out 100 pieces of skin from his arms and danced for 24 hours. His painful arms were swollen and blood oozed down and onto the ground.

Sioux Indians do a sun dance by George Satlin 1835-1837

After a day of dancing, he had an unusual vision. Soldiers "as thick as grasshoppers," riding into an Indian camp upside down. He then saw the same men falling from the sky to crash dead on the ground. It was a sign of victory. The warriors cheered and screamed a fearsome war-whoop. Now, they began searching for the soldiers.

Battle of the Rosebud

On the early morning of June 17, General Crooke's column stopped to brew coffee on the banks of Rosebud creek. Nobody suspected that 500 warriors were preparing for a charge.

Warriors attack at the Rosebud by Charles Stanley (Library of Congress)

Chief Crazy Horse and his braves executed a swift attack on the unsuspecting soldiers. Crooke and his troops were shocked that the Indians weren't fleeing. The cavalrymen only had enough time to scramble on their horses and fire a few shots at the warriors. Crooke's command soon fell apart. After a day worth of desperate fighting, about 30 soldiers were dead and another 50 wounded. Crooke was stunned by the ferocity of the attack. The following day, he retreated to Fort Fetterman in defeat.

Shortly after the victory, Sitting Bull took his village north to a river named the Little Bighorn (a small tributary of the Bighorn River). The size of the Indian migration left an easy trail for the Army Scouts to follow. The Indians celebrated their victory for six days at the banks of the Little Bighorn. More than 1,000 lodges, 7,000 people, and 2,000 warriors made up a three-mile-long camp. It was by far the largest known Indian encampment on the plains.

General Custer's death struggle by Henry Steinegger (Library of Congress)

On June 21, Colonel Gibbon's column met General Terry's column at the mouth of the Yellowstone River. Nobody was aware of Crooke's retreat. Instead of waiting for Crooke, General Terry decided to attack without him.

Terry would send Colonel Gibbon to the beginning of the Little Bighorn; Custer would take his 7th cavalry South then push North, through the Little Bighorn and Rosebud Creek, to drive any Indians towards Gibbon's soldiers. Terry was confident that his plan would work.

On June 22, Custer and 600 troopers of the 7th cavalry left General Terry's column. As Custer prepared to leave, Colonel Gibbon yelled out to him, "Now Custer, don't be greedy; wait for us." Custer responded by saying, "No, I will not."

Custer and his cavalrymen would ride over 100 miles into southern Montana's harsh terrain. The first day, Custer only traveled 12 miles before making camp on Rosebud creek. The next day, Custer broke his camp early, and he sent his chief scout, Mitch Boyer, and his other Crow scouts ahead of his troops to scout the landscape. Custer's cavalry then stumbled upon evidence of a vast trail where pony tracks crisscrossed in every direction. The scouts agreed that the village would be enormous, and they advised the Colonel not to take on such a large force alone. Custer pondered their advice, and then he said, "Follow the trail." They rode 35 miles before night fell.

The following day, Mitch Boyer discovered two buffalo skulls and a blond scalp tied to a tree. The scalp was found to belong to trooper Augustus Stoker, who had been killed in an Indian raid a month before. Unknown to Boyer, this was the exact place where Sitting Bull had seen a vision of Custer's defeat. Each trooper rode past it in silence, perhaps they had a premonition of the tragic events of the following day.

"Call of the Bugle," by J.K. Ralston (John W. Painter)

Battle of the Little Bighorn

The following day was Sunday, June 25. Custer was camped more than 20 miles away from the Indian village in the Little Bighorn valley. While his soldiers cooked breakfast, Mitch Boyer and his Crow scouts peered through the lenses of an old telescope on a ridge 5 miles from Custer's camp. They could barely make out a distant pony herd and smoke from hundreds of morning campfires.

The commander of the scouts, Lieutenant Charles Varnum, was handed the telescope and told to search for what looked like "worms crawling on the grass". Varnum could only see the distant Montana hills, but he trusted his scouts. Varnum urgently sent word to Custer about the village.

"The Last Command" by Kirk Stirnweis 2001

Custer did not delay. He immediately galloped, as fast as he could, to the ridge. The Colonel anxiously began scanning the landscape for the village. Much like Varnum, Custer expected to see hundreds of teepees, but he couldn't see anything. Frustrated, Custer said, "I've got about as good eyes as anybody, and I can't see any village, Indians, or anything else."

Mitch Boyer assured him saying, "Well, General, if you don't find more Indians in that valley than you ever saw together, you can hang me." Custer swore and uttered, "It would do a... sight of good to hang you, wouldn't it?" He then rode back to camp, fetched a pair of binoculars and returned. This time, he made out soft fluffy objects on the distant valley floor. He was convinced; this was the village.

When Custer returned to camp, an officer told him that his men found some Indians trying to open a box of hardtack dropped by the mule trains the day before. Custer was furious; he didn't want the Indians to know about his presence. He feared that they were already scattering. It was now or never.

Crow scouts who survived the battle gather at Custer's grave in 1908.

Before Custer broke camp, he reorganized his men into four battalions. One battalion of 120 men would be led by Captain Frederick Benteen (companies D, H, and K). Another battalion of 175 men would be led by Major Marcus Reno (companies A, G, and M). The third battalion of 221 men was led by Custer (companies C, E, F, I, and L), but his command would be split into 2 wings. The left-wing was led by Captain George Yates, and the right-wing was led by Captain Myles Keogh. Another 100 men would be left to guard the pack train which was falling behind.

Major Marcus Reno (Denver Public Library Digital Collections)

Custer planned to send Benteen and his battalion to the left, on several distant ridges, to cut off any Indians attempting to escape. Major Reno would attack the village head-on and drive the Indians out, and Custer promised to support him. Before Benteen galloped away, he asked Custer "Hadn't we better keep the regiment together, General? If this is as big a camp as they say, we'll need every man we have." Custer ordered him to obey his command, so Benteen rode off. He would never see Custer alive again.

Captain Frederick Benteen (Library of Congress)

Custer and Reno followed the Little Bighorn for about two hours until they reached one single teepee, referred to as the 'lone teepee'. Custer looked inside. He saw the remains of a warrior named Old She-Bear who was killed during the battle of the Rosebud.

A civilian scout named Fred Girard yelled out to Custer, "There are your Indians General, running like devils!" Custer looked for himself to see a band of about 50-100 Indians fleeing towards the village. Custer had been spotted. He quickly galloped to Reno and ordered him to make his attack telling him, "The Indians are about two miles and a half ahead. They are on the jump. Go forward as fast as you think proper, and charge them wherever you find them, and I will support you."

Reno Routed by Olaf Carl Seltzer (Glcrease Museum)

In the village, the Indians were not expecting a battle on a hot and lazy afternoon. Many of them were eating lunch or swimming in the river. A group of Sioux boys had spotted the soldiers from a way off, and now they sprinted into the camp yelling "Soldiers! Soldiers!" The Indians were shocked; they didn't know that soldiers were nearby. Stunned warriors scrambled for their weapons and ponies, and women began taking down their lodges. Sitting Bull knew that this would be the battle he prophesied.

Retreat of Reno's Command by Amos Bad Heart Bull (1900)

Reno's mounted cavalry splashed across the river south of the camp onto an open plain where they prepared to make a charge on the Indian encampment. The soldiers lined up their horses for the first attack. Reno signaled his bugler to sound a charge, and the 175 troopers sprang into a gallop towards the village. Simultaneously, hundreds of fierce warriors rode out to fight them.

Reno realized that his command was at the risk of being overrun, so he stopped his advance to form a thin skirmish line. Trooper James Turley did not hear the order, and he bolted his horse into the Indian village. His body was never found.

The soldiers began a withering fire, cutting down advancing braves, and clipping the tops of teepees. Every fourth man held the reigns of his comrade's nervous horses. Outnumbered nearly 5 to 1 Reno's soldiers fought bravely against stacked odds. While Reno fired at advancing warriors, he searched the surrounding hills for any evidence of Custer's reinforcements.

Reno's soldiers retreat across the Little Bighorn River by Martin Pate (Friends of the Little Bighorn Battlefield)

The major knew that his situation was hopeless, so he retreated to a nearby grove of cottonwood trees near the river bank. The Indian braves, led by the fearless Chief Crazy Horse, continued to pursue the panicked soldiers.

The timber was a natural defensive position. Trees and logs offered protection of the mass of desperate soldiers. The screaming Indians galloped through the trees, cutting down running cavalrymen.

In the heat of the fighting, several warriors crawled through the brush and fired their guns at the troopers. One bullet struck Custer's favorite scout, Chief Bloody Knife, in the head; his blood and brains splattered across Reno's face. Reno's composure vanished in a flash of panic.

Troopers Being Driven Across the River by Amos Bad Heart Bull (Private Collection The Stapleton Collection The Bridgeman Art Library.)

A white scout George Herendeen remembered, "There was little firing for some minutes, and then we received a volley from the bushes... The volley killed Bloody Knife and one soldier. I heard the soldier call out as he fell, 'Oh! My God, I have got it". The horrified major ordered his men to mount, but then he ordered them to dismount and then mount again. Reno then screamed out, "Any of you men who wish to live, make your escape – follow me!"

The withdrawal soon became a rout. The famed scout "Lonesome" Charley Reynolds was unhorsed and killed in an attempt to catch up with his retreating companions. Lieutenant

Donald McIntosh was also unhorsed, surrounded, and beat to death by about 20 Indians.

Reno and his men then splashed across the river. The Indians followed in hot pursuit. The crossing was not a ford and was one of the worst places the soldiers could have crossed. Reno's adjutant, Lieutenant Benjamin Hodgeson, was shot off his horse, but he was able to grab the stirrup of a fleeing trooper, which pulled him through the cold water. Once on the other side, however, he was killed by an arrow. Hodgeson's ghost is still said to haunt the battlefield at night.

The exhausted troopers then scrambled to climb a steep bluff. The men even grabbed their horse's tails to pull themselves up. At the top, Reno and the rest of the survivors fought off of the warriors. The hill is today known as Reno Hill. Many of the Indians left to fight Custer, and others stopped to mutilate the dead.

"I was very small, and I had no chance to shoot anyone... We stopped on a flat and everyone would get a soldier and strip him and put on his clothes for himself. We took everything they had-pistols, guns, ammunition, etc.... we saw a kicking soldier and a man came up and said, 'Boy, get off and scalp him,' So I got off and began to take my knife. Of course the soldier had short hair so I started to cut it off probably it hurt him because he began to grind his teeth. After I did this I took my pistol out and shot him in the forehead." - Black Elk

Panic turned to horror as Reno and his troops realized the extent of their losses. About 50 dead or dying cavalry men or one-third of his command littered their retreat. Reno's remaining men were safe on the bluff, for now.

'Custer's Last Stand' by Edgar S. Paxson (Buffalo Bill Center of the West)

Custer's Fight

Shortly after sending Reno into the valley, Custer and his command rode up the steep high bluffs opposite of the Indian camp. Here, Custer saw the entire village; he was stunned at the sight of thousands of teepees. He could make out Reno and his skirmish line far below. It was the first time Custer saw the entire village, and it was the first time he realized that he was desperately short of men.

Custer turned to his adjutant, Lieutenant William Crooke, and ordered him to write a message and send it to Benteen. Crooke scribbled down, "Benteen. Come on. Big village. Be Quick. Bring Packs. P.[S.] Bring pacs." Crooke gave the message to a trumpeter named John Martin, an Italian who could barely speak English.

After Martin galloped away to Benteen, Custer led his troops down a ravine named Medicine Trail Coulee.

"The Last Stand" by Frederic Remington

Benteen's battalion was still on the ridges Custer sent him to earlier. At around 3:35, Benteen was greeted by Custer's trumpeter, John Martin, who trotted anxiously to deliver his message. Martin proudly informed Benteen that the Indians had "skedaddled". Although the message said to "Be quick", the captain was in no rush, so he decided to patiently wait for the packs. This would be an awful mistake.

Custer's Last Stand by Theodore Pitman (Little Bighorn National Monument)

A civilian, Boston Custer, left the slow-moving pack train to join his older brother's battalion. He met Custer and his troops riding down the Medicine Trail Coulee. When asked about Benteen's whereabouts, Boston told him that he passed Benteen's Battalion a few miles back. This made Custer believe that Benteen was already on his way, so he halted his command and waited.

As Custer waited, Mitch Boyer went ahead to spy on the Indian's movements. He returned with alarming news; Reno's battalions had been defeated and were being slaughtered as they crossed the river. Custer needed to attack or risk Reno's entire battalion. He decided that his battalion would make a false attack on the village to lure Indians away from Reno.

Custer quickly divided his command into 2 wings. The left-wing was led by Captain George Yates, and the right-wing was led by Captain Myles Keogh. Custer and Yates would take the left-wing and attack on the village then swoop back around and meet Keogh's right-wing that would be stationed on a ridge.

Companies F and E retreat from Medicine Tail Coulee by Martin Pate (Friends Of The Little Bighorn Battlefield)

As Custer prepared for the attack, he yelled out, "Hurrah boys, we've got them! We'll finish them up and then go home to our station." His bugler then sounded a charge. The soldiers let out a cheer, then thundered down towards the village. Warriors under Chief Crazy Horse, Chief Gall, and Chief Lame White Man left Reno's fight to engage Custer.

Custer's Last Stand by Charles Russell (Gilcrease Museum)

Custer's soldiers were stunned at the sight of screaming warriors riding towards them. He then turned back around towards the right-wing, waiting for them on the ridge. The attack did draw warriors from Reno, but now hundreds of Indians were racing after the cavalrymen.

The Indian warrior Low Dog remembered, "They come on us like a thunderbolt. I never before nor since saw men so brave and fearless as those white warriors. We retreated until our men got all together and then we charged upon them I called to my men, 'this is a good day to die: follow me.' We massed our men, and that no man should fall back, every man whipped another man's horse and we rushed right upon them."

Custer's Last Stand by Nick Eggenhofer (1925)

When Custer arrived, Captain Keogh was skirmishing a handful of Indians, but they were no threat. Custer then moved north and stopped on a hill. Today it is known as Calhoun Hill, named after Custer's brother in law who would die there.

Custer could see women and children were fleeing from the village. At the battle of the Washita years earlier, Custer captured women and children hostages. The Cheyenne Indians wouldn't risk their women and children, so they didn't attack. He was sure the same thing would happen here.

Lame White Man's charge by Martin Pate (Friends Of The Little Bighorn Battlefield.)

Custer decided to split his forces again. Keogh's wing would defend Calhoun Hill. Yates and Custer would take the left-wing across the river and capture the women and children. As Custer left the hill, Keogh had no idea that they would never meet again.

Keogh ordered his troops to dismount and form a skirmish line. As the Indians began their attack, Keogh screamed out, "Fire!" The entire hill lit up in smoke. Indians hid in nearby gullies where they fired arrows from a distance in complete cover.

Capt. Myles W. Keogh, Co. I, 7th U.S. Cavalry. (Little Bighorn National Monument.)

A squaw named Antelope Women remembered, "A band of the soldiers on the ridge mounted their horses and came riding in a gallop down the broad coulee toward the river... Lame White Man, the bravest Cheyenne warrior chief, stayed in hiding close where the small band of soldiers got off their horses. From there he called to the young men, and they began creeping and dodging back to him. The Ogallala Sioux chiefs also called to their young men... Within a few minutes there were many hundreds of warriors along the gullies all around those soldiers."

The bravest Cheyenne Chief, Lame White Man, led his young braves in a charge up Calhoun Hill. Dozens of warriors were shot down including Lame White Man himself, but they were soon engaged in brutal hand to hand fighting. The soldiers who had not been killed, abandoned the hill and ran for their lives. Keogh and his cavalrymen bunched together in small desperate attempts to resist until help arrived, nearly all of the soldiers were killed. Keogh's body was found in one of these groups. Only a lucky few were able to escape to the rest of Custer's command.

The Custer Fight by Charles Russell (Library of Congress)

A Cheyenne warrior named Yellow Nose captured an abandoned cavalry flag. With it, he raced forward on his horse and touched one of the frantic soldiers. This was known as "count coup". For the Indians, it was a great honor for someone to touch their enemy in the thick of battle. Yellow Nose's daring actions would earn him great respect for the rest of his life, and it was one of the proudest moments for the Cheyenne during the battle.

"Indians hid behind little rolls. The soldiers were on one side of the hill and the Indians on the other, a slight rise between them. While they were lying there shooting at one another, Crazy Horse came up on horseback- with an eagle horn- and rode between the two parties. The soldiers all fired at once, but didn't hit him. The Indians got the idea the soldiers' guns were empty and charged immediately on the soldiers." -Red Feather

At the same time, Custer and the left-wing galloped towards the river. Custer could still see dozens of women and children fleeing out of the camp in terror. If he could find a crossing, the battle would be over. Custer took his troops to the banks of the Little Bighorn in an attempt to find a ford, but the ground was to muddy to cross. At the same time, the Indians knew where to cross the river and hundreds of braves galloped through the water to fight Custer. Custer must have been shocked to see the endless stream of warriors coming to fight him, so he gave the order to fall back.

Custer and his men were soon in a desperate retreat. Troopers were getting shot or clubbed out of the saddle. He was able to rally his men on a ridge to fire back at their pursuers. It was evolving into a desperate fight, but Custer must have been sure that Benteen was still on his way.

Things went worse for Custer when women with blankets scared off most of his horses. He had lost his mobility, Custer was now on the defense. His only chance was to fight until help arrived. Custer and his 30-40 survivors left the ridge and went to a hill; now known today as Last Stand Hill.

Custer's Last Fight by Otto Becker (1889)

On top of the hill, Custer and his men were surrounded. The soldiers fired at the daring Indian warriors, who were attacking in every direction. In the chaos, Crazy Horse single-handedly charged at a line of soldiers. This encouraged his warriors, and they rushed forward to finish them off.

The cavalrymen were so desperate that they shot their horses to use as barricades. Gunfire and howling Indians only added to the chaos that was unfolding before Custer and his men.

"I charged in. A tall, well-built soldier with yellow hair and mustache saw me coming and tried to bluff me, aiming his rifle at me. But when I rushed him, he threw his rifle at me without shooting. I dodged it. We grabbed each other and wrestled there in the dust and smoke. It was like fighting in a fog. This soldier was very strong and brave... He hit me with his fists on the jaw and shoulders, then grabbed my long braids with both

hands, pulled my face close and tried to bite my nose off... Finally I broke free. He drew his pistol. I wrenched it out of his hand and struck him with it three or four times on the head, knocked him over, shot him in the head, and fired at his heart." -White Bull

With Their Boots On: Battle of Little Big Horn by Michael Schreck (2002)

Custer must have been heroic as ever on his final moments on Last Stand Hill. His body was found with bullet wounds in his left temple and the chest. One of the most famous Indian fighters in the west was dead.

Mitch Boyer and a handful of others broke away from Last Stand Hill and frantically ran towards the river. Warriors galloped after them in pursuit. Suicide boys (warriors who promised to die for their tribe) are credited for charging in on the fleeing troopers and killing most of them, including Mitch Boyer.

Gen. George A. Custer by Mathew Brady (The U.S. National Archives)

Only about a dozen troopers were able to make it to a gorge known as Deep Ravine where they were fired upon from above. It was at Deep Ravine where the true last stand took place. Every man from Custer's battalion was killed.

Benteen goes to Reno

Major Reno's men huddled together on the top of Reno Hill. Stunned, their commander was searching for his adjutant and good friend, Lieutenant Hodgeson. Little did he know that his friend had been killed during the river crossing.

Trooper William Taylor remembered, "Major Reno was walking around in an excited manner, He had lost his hat... and had bound a red handkerchief around his head, which gave him a rather peculiar and unmilitary appearance."

At the same time Captain Benteen and his battalion slowly trotted towards Reno Hill. The major was so relieved that they had come. Benteen had been summoned by the note Custer sent to him.

One of Benteen's company commanders, Captain Thomas Weir, could hear shooting from Custer's fight. He knew that Custer could not hold off against so many warriors. Weir asked Benteen for permission to go and help Custer, but Benteen denied it. Instead, he ordered his troopers to dig rifle pits. Weir was shocked at Benteen's decision. He shook his head, and without orders, the captain took his company towards the firing.

He didn't travel far when he halted his company to observed giant clouds of smoke coming from Last Stand Hill. Through binoculars, Weir saw Indians shooting at things on the ground. What he was witnessing was likely the final moments of the battle. He was there for only a few minutes until dozens of Indian braves spotted him, and they chased them back to Reno Hill. No more attempts to relieve Custer were made.

Corporal Charles A. Windolph (1876)

Later that night the exhausted soldiers scraped breast-works out of dirt. They could hear the distant cheers of victorious howling Indians. Every man would have wondered about Custer. Charles Windolph remembered, "The quick Montana twilight settled down on us... welcome as the darkness was, it brought a penetrating feeling of fear and uncertainty of what tomorrow might bring. We felt terribly alone on that dangerous hilltop. We were a million miles from nowhere. And death was all around us."

The next morning, the soldiers were awakened by distant gunshots. As the hot sun blazed upon them, wounded soldiers began begging for water. Benteen called for volunteers to go to the river and fetch water. Four marksmen, including Private Windolph, and 20 others went towards the river and fetched water. The 24 men would each earn the Medal of Honor.

His Brother's Keeper by Mark Churms (2003)

While Indian warriors kept the troopers pinned on the hill, the entire village quickly left the valley. With them went the spoils from Custer's mutilated troops. The next morning, General Terry and the main column arrived at the battlefield. The soldiers went out to see the fate of Custer and his men.

They were shocked to find their comrades bodies stripped of their clothing and mutilated beyond recognition. Last Stand Hill was covered in 42 mutilated bodies, and 39 dead horses.

Bones at Little Big Horn 1876 by Stanly Morrow (Library of Congress)

Custer was found stripped of his uniform, but he was neither mutilated nor scalped. He was lying on top of a dead trooper and horse. Next to him were 17 shells from his Remington Rifle. Years later, two Cheyenne women explained that they pierced his ears with needles, so he could listen to the Indians and his broken promises in the next life.

Not far away was Custer's younger brother Tom. He had been mutilated so badly that he could only be identified by an eagle tattoo on his arm. An Indian brave, named Rain in the Face, boasted that he cut out his heart and ate it. Custer's adjutant, William Cooke, had been shot full of arrows, and his sideburns had been scalped.

Comanche by John C. H. Grabill (, Library of Congress)

Also on Custer Hill was Boston Custer, a trumpeter, and Sargent Hughes Farther, the flag bearer. Assistant Surgeon George Lord was only identified by a blue shirt he was wearing. His Surgeon Kit was recovered by the Indians and given to the Army's medical museum. Trooper Vincent Charlie broke off from Last Stand Hill and was found with a bullet wound in his hip and a stick jammed down his throat. Many others could not be identified.

No soldier in Custer's battalion survived the battle of the Little Bighorn. All 210 men under him were killed. Another 40-50 soldiers were killed during the Reno valley fight. It is estimated that only about 60-100 Indian braves died during the fighting. The sole survivor from Custer's command was Captain Keogh's horse, Comanche. He was found with dozens of wounds. He died 15 years later with a military funeral and full military honors.

The Sioux Reservation

Sitting Bull and Buffalo Bill by William Notman (Library of Congress)

The news of Custer's demise spread like a wildfire. Throughout America, newspapers printed dozens of articles about the terrible "Custer Massacre". The newspapers demonized the Indians, calling them ruthless savages who butchered the gallant soldiers of the 7th Cavalry. The public was shocked. How could the most respected commander of the Civil War and his entire command be wiped out by a bunch of savages?

Lt. Col. George Armstrong Custer. By José María Mora (Glenwood Swanson Collection)

After the battle, Congress sent hundreds more soldiers west to force the Indians on the reservation. A battalion formed called "Custer's Avengers". They swore to avenge Custer at all cost. The troopers burned down villages and hunted down the inhabitants. Sitting Bull and his followers fled to Canada. Chief Crazy Horse and other warriors who fought in the battle returned to the reservation.

Crazy Horse was killed by prison guards a year later. The reservation was cut down to a shadow of its former size. The government took away the sacred Black Hills and 40 million acres of Indian land. Sitting Bull returned to the United States and surrendered himself to the reservation.

"I wish it to be remembered that I was the last man of my tribe to surrender my rifle, this day have I given it to you."   -Sitting Bull

The Battlefield Today

Today the battlefield is covered in markers that stand where the soldiers and Indians fell during the battle. A memorial was placed on Last Stand Hill commemorating the men who died there. In the valley far below lays the small town of Garryowen (named after the 7th cavalry's marching song).

In 1984 a team of archeologist recovered a skull fragment of the upper teeth, nose, and left eye buried in the battlefield. The teeth showed evidence of pipe smoking, and the individual received a gruesome blow to the face. The bone was compared to a photograph which fit perfectly. It was the photograph of Mitch Boyer. It was a tragic reminder of the human cost in the battle.

In 1926, over 50,000 people gathered to the very spot where Reno made his first skirmish line, where it all began. They gathered here to remember the battle and to commemorate an unknown soldier who was found by workers building US Hwy 87. The soldier was buried with a hatchet which represents peace. More than 50 years after the battle of the Little Bighorn, there was finally peace in the hills of Southern Montana

"If I were an Indian I often think that I would greatly prefer to cast my lot among those of my people who adhered to the free open plains, rather than submit to the confined limits of a reservation.

-Colonel George Armstrong Custer

George Armstrong Custer in field uniform by Mathew Brady (Library of Congress) 1865

Works Cited

Allison, Kurz and. *Custer's Last Stand*. – Courtesy Library of Congress –.

Andrews, George L. *Major General George A. Custer*. National Archives & Records Administration .

Army, United States. *Crow scouts*. Little Bighorn Battlefield National Monument.

Barry, David Francis. *Marcus Reno*. Denver Public Library Digital Collections.

Battle of the Little Bighorn. 16 August 2019. 20 August 2019. <https://en.wikipedia.org/wiki/Battle_of_the_Little_Bighorn>.

Battle of the Little Bighorn. 2 December 2009. 20 August 2019. <https://www.history.com/topics/native-american-history/battle-of-the-little-bighorn>.

Becker, F. Otto. *Custer's Last Fight*.

Brady, Mathew. *Gen. George A. Custer* . The U.S. National Archives. *Mathew Brady Photographs of Civil War-Era Personalities and Scenes,*. 1863.

Brady, Mathew B. *Gen. Geo. A. Custer*. Library of Congress.

Brady, Mathew. *General George A. Custer*. Brady National Photographic Art Gallery .

Buffalo, Amos Bad Heart. *Troopers Being Driven Across the River*. Amos Bad Heart Buffalo Private Collection The Stapleton Collection The Bridgeman Art Library.

Bull, Amos Bad Heart. *Retreat of Reno's Command.*

Captain Frederick William Benteen . 1871.

Carson, Jim. *Custer on the ridge.*

Churms, Mark. *His Brother's Keeper* .

Curtis, Edward Sheriff. *Sioux Chiefs.* library of congress.

Deming, E. W. *Battle of the Little Big Horn.* the Buffalo Bill Museum.

Eber, Elk. *Custer's Last Battle.* Little Bighorn Battlefield National Monument.

Eggenhofer, Nick. *CUSTER'S LAST STAND.*

Goff., Orlando Scott. *Officers and wives at Ft. Lincoln, 1873.* Little BIghorn National Monument, 1873.

Grabill, John C. H. *Comanche.* John C. H. Grabill Collection, Library of Congress.

Heinz, Ralph. *Trumpeter Fisher and Lt. Hodgson June 25, 1876.* Pritzker Military Museum & Library . *Hardin, Montana : Custer Battlefield Preservation Committee.* n.d.

Henry, Steinegger. *General Custer's death struggle. The battle of the Little Big Horn.* Library of Congress.

Llingworth. *Custer's Bear.*

Locke, H.R. *LITTLE BIGHORN BATTLEFIELD.* Library of Congress, Deadwood S.D.

Martin, Sergeant John. *Benteen. Come on. Big Village. Be quick. Bring Packs. P.S. Bring Packs.* . West Point Military Academy.

McCarthy, Frank C. *THE LAST STAND: LITTLE BIG HORN.*

Mora, José María. *Lt. Col. George Armstrong Custer*. Glenwood Swanson Collection.

Morrow, S.J. *Bones at Little Big Horn 1876*. Library of Congress, Yankton, S.D.

N/A. *Capt. Myles W. Keogh, Co. I, 7th U.S. Cavalry*. Little Bighorn Battlefield.

N/A. *Little Bighorn Battlefield National Monument*. 2011.

Panzieri, Peter. *LITTLE BIG HORN 1876 Custer's Last Stand*. Great Britain: Osprey Publishing, 1995.

Pate, Martin. *Companies F and E retreat from Medicine Tail Coulee*. Friends Of The Little Bighorn Battlefield.

Pate, Martin. *Lame White Man's charge*. Friends Of The Little Bighorn Battlefield.

Pate, Martin. *Reno's soliders retreat across the Little Bighorn River*. Friends Of The Little Bighorn Battlefield.

Pate, Martin. *Soldiers on Weir Point just before forced to retreat back to the Reno-Benteen Defense Site*. Friends Of The Little Bighorn Battlefield. . , . .

Paxson, Edgar Samuel. *Custer's Last Stand*. Buffalo Bill Center of the West.

Pitman, Theodore B. *Custers Last Stand*. Little Bighorn Battlefield National Monument.

Poincot, A. *US Casualty Marker Battle of the Little Bighorn*. 2017.

Pollart, Thomas. *General George Armstrong Custer* . Library of Congress.

Ralston, J.K. "*Call of the Bugle,*" . American Indian Photography Collection of John W. Painter (1929-2008).

Remington, Frederic. *"The Last Stand"*.

Russell, Charles Marion. *Custer's Last Stand*. Gilcrease Museum.

Russell, Charles Marion. The Custer Fight. Library of Congress. 1903.

Satlin, George. *The Sun Dance*.

Schmidt, Eric von. *Here Fell Custer*. Friends Of The Little Bighorn Battlefield.

Schmidt, Harold Von. *Custer's Last Stand*.

Schrebogel, Charles. *Tomahawk and sabre*. Library of Congress.

Schreck, Michael. *With Their Boots On: Battle of Little Big Horn*.

Schreyvogel, Charles. *Surrounded*. Gilcrease Museum.

Seltzer, Olaf Carl. *Reno Routed*. Glcrease Museum.

Son, William Notman and. *Sitting Bull and Buffalo Bill*. Library of Congress.

Stanley, Charles St.G. *Sioux charging at Battle of Rosebud*. Library of Congress's Prints and Photographs division.

Stein, R. Conard. *Cornerstones of Freedom The Story of The Little Bighorn*. Chicago: Childrens Press, Chicago, 1983.

Stirnweis, Kirk. *The Last Command*.

Thomas, Andy. *Yellow Nose Count Coup At Little Big Horn*.

unknown. *Corporal Charles A. Windolph*.

unknown. *Frederick William Benteen*. Library of Congress . 1888

Unknown. *Mitch Boyer*.

unknown. *Supply wagons*. National Archives.

Walker, Paul Robert. *Remember Little Bighorn: Indians, Soldiers, and Scouts Tell Their Stories.* Washington DC: National Geographic, 2006.

weldon, catherine. *Portrait Of Sioux Chief Sitting Bull.* Hulton Archive.

Printed in Great Britain
by Amazon